*For Phyllis Walden
old buddy,
John K
11/10/95*

the chinkapin oak

poems 1993-1995

by John Knoepfle

*and with love from
Jackie, Christmas 1995*

ROSEHILL PRESS
Springfield

The publication of this book is partially funded
through City Arts, a program of the Springfield Area
Arts Council and the City of Springfield.

Copyright © 1995 by John Knoepfle
All rights reserved.

Cover photo of the chinkapin oak
in Lincoln Memorial Garden:
Ginny Lee of Springfield, Illinois

Printer:
United Graphics of Mattoon, Illinois

Publisher:
Rosehill Press
545 South Feldkamp Avenue
Springfield, Illinois 62704-1644

Library of Congress Catalog Card No. 95-71132
ISBN 0-9646037-4-8

Manufactured in the United States of America
on recycled paper using soy inks

for Rosie Richmond [1944-1994]

and her friends

poems in this collection have appeared, in various stages of development, or will appear, in the following periodicals, papers, and journals: *Farmer's Market, Illinois Issues, Auburn Citizen, Borderlands: Texas Poetry Review, The State Journal-Register, The Other Side, Illinois Times, New Letters, Green Fuse Poetry, The Illinois Architectural and Historical Review, AMI Illinois State Line, New Virginia Review, Fine Madness, Stiletto, IWI Newsletter, Mississippi Valley Review, Another Chicago Magazine, River Styx, East West: A Poetry Annual, River King Poetry Supplement, Clockwatch Review, The Lower Lip, Illinois Native Plant Society: Central Chapter Newsletter, International Quarterly, The Sept* and *Springhouse*

contents

what we begin we begin again   *3*
after epiphany and all   *5*
the poet at seventy-two   *6*
three for rosie
   recovering the angelic past   *7*
   at lincoln library   *7*
   hearing kathleen battle singing   *9*
a day of recollection   *10*
presidents day springfield   *11*
reclaiming the light   *14*
peace store   *15*
goethes dog would have been sublime   *17*
for bill stafford and pete simpson   *18*
the mahotella queens and mahlathini   *19*
after the pancakes and the shouting   *20*
rendering the maple syrup   *21*
the sorrows of the marsh arabs
   and the mind running on   *22*
day of the butterfly conference   *23*
march and the crocus cluster   *28*
there were choices   *30*
AMI at the hilton   *31*
polycarp   *33*
chanting the circle: lines for earth week
   and the "greenman is coming" pageant in
   carpenter park   *34*
leland hotel a collage   *36*
humanities lecture at the governors mansion
   on the feast day of the venerable bede   *38*
after the nuclear assurances   *39*
and now the four seasons
   this day that was summer   *40*
   autumn in illinois   *40*
   beyond the cold solstice   *41*
   spring tokens   *42*

was a good party *43*
lines for the fourth *44*
washington park carillon festival *46*
a little song for sugar cubes *47*
poems from vacations
   north carolina outer banks *48*
   south of fort worth *49*
   on top of the world *49*
   beneath kennesaw mountain *50*
   rafting in denali *51*
chinkapin oak lincoln
   memorial garden *52*
poet in a small place *54*
oak ridge cemetery *55*
considering the budget with isaiah *56*
program meeting *57*
poem at the full september moon *58*
labor day this hundred years *59*
double puppet *61*
gandhiji *62*
dark spaces thoughts on all
   souls day *63*
bagatelles *64*
some words for the lighting of the
   christmas tree in the auburn
   illinois town square *69*
perspectives on aging lines for
   an anniversary *71*
in the december gallery *74*
now the last is the first again *76*
waking at two a.m. *78*

what we begin we begin again

the great orbit complete once more
through the hours of our babylon
our months of saint gregory
a day now for the usual chance of rain
temperature into the high thirties

we abide in a promise
not knowing what will be ahead of us
but these are the hours
for temple bells their sonorous greeting
a toast for the gods with rice wine

and three million in brazil
went to the copacabana it was that time
for washing their feet in the ocean
cleansing the bad actions of the year gone
and a half million frenchmen
sprayed champagne on the champs elysees

the new emperor and empress of japan
have moved into the imperial palace
but michiko longs for her old home
the window where she could watch the sunset
and akihito pens a solemn haiku
for the king of belgium his friend
grieving that mans empty palace

but I will not go on
there was so much to be spoken of
so much that is lost
so many friends we will not see again

I have begun with everything
and with nothing only a handful of words
and with these we conjure
a new shape for the world
as octavio says in another poem
and so it seems right to say here
a prayer for the mouths that will reform these words
the eyes transfiguring them
this being in the nature of the new year

after epiphany and all

the three kings were generous
and meanwhile the unworthy sandal
his day has come and gone
time to put aside the ornaments
face into that brain numbing west wind
january offers our mortality

looking at these words now
I understand old jane how she
always wanted her lines
would be better than they were

you have to have courage I guess
or whatever old bill had who would say
why it is not so hard you just
lower your standards
and he would tell you
they were bread and butter poems
could do a whole notebook full
flying from portland to st louis

so here are these meager lines
I do not think they will make you fat
and anyway when the light comes
you will see the bones in your hands
and you will not need them

the poet at seventy-two

owl on a branch of sycamore
where the river washes shallow
fisherman in waders
heart firing its roman candles
expenditure of so much time
soot of the hours so many
ashes in the memory now
sound of a wooden flute
a friend practicing his scales
a widening place in the evening
neon display on a barn side
oh yes I have pilfered the hours
eel sucking on life an alien
loving this worlds hayrack
soul always expectant always
ready for its prom date
why dont I confess it my life
was so many warm colors
comforters like great amiable dogs
or colts frolicking in pastures
this is a myth you understand
someone elses life not mine
mine an unaccountable survival
a coral formation something hoarded
and why now these halcyon days
I cannot tell you something measured
under orion before gray dawn
mischief still in these hands eyes
a thousand pardons oh pardon

three for rosie

1

recovering the angelic past

ricardo wondered about it
an angel getting into his poem
remembered a schoolchild prayer
or rather couldnt remember it
I volunteered saint michael
but it was not that prayer and
I would have tried for raphael
but there was no such prayer
no healing shield for lovers
so we didnt get far with angels
then at the breakfast
suddenly I could chant the line
angel of god my guardian dear
and they sat still and waited
while I thirsted in the dry
limits of my second grade eden
then peg fresh as apricots
recited the whole thing
well we were impressed and rosie
who grew up in the projects
and did not know this prayer
took a moment to write it down
said it was better than zen

2

at lincoln library

childrens exhibit amazing
colors oh the third graders
already they hazard picasso
but I do not think they know their
maritain those fractured profiles

the way angels see men he wrote
so many faces contours in collages
the human lurking in these masks

this morning the chill sunshine
maria is reading from gwendolyn brooks
for television and peg is hostess
an old series here on access 4
she was always off the wall with rosie
cohosting an easy partnership and now
yesterday the rabbi walking another
world for rosie his rich deep shalom
and after that our shovels of dirt
she was our rosie used to come here
writing her droll stories

a young man who works in the library
recognizes maria she was his teacher
from carbondale his face quickens
like sunrise in a mist hung morning
I tell him a small world yes he says

maria and peg warm to the poems
chocolate mabbie the bean eaters
tracing a life cycle gwendolyns
preoccupations her generosity
I have lived with peg these 37 years
I know what it is costing her this morning
but now with maria it seems they are
girls at a junior high blackboard
conspirators sharing a playground secret as they
brush the surface of lines for prisoners
uncovering the deep prayer in it

when their session is over
I walk down thick carpeted steps
I want to ask the reference librarian
how much does the human heart weigh
she looks it up says why yes it says
between nine and twelve ounces
we stare at each other in disbelief

3

hearing kathleen battle singing

rosie you were everybodys
best friend and we would have
held you so fiercely when your time came
but you slipped through
the bones in our hands

and the world is in his hands
woods and the waters
beasts of the field
all the sorrows there ever were
held in those crippled hands

and you rosie in his hands

a day of recollection

somehow we are able to say
strangled love yes but love
here in this unfamiliar room
true believers
blind eyed and squinting
beneath tall shafts of light
teachers until we failed

where have we come from
together now
fifteen pairs of glasses
the room stone cold
footsteps echoing on tiled floors
clock climbing the hour

and now these yellow roses
the hands on shoulders
book with the red and black letters
"come, here is the page"
ceramic cup and the loaves

presidents day springfield

    1

I order a pineapple drink
the glass has a cherry smear
and I send it back
tell them this was not my lipstick

three bean salad the chef
has a good eye with his
garbanzo and red kidney
lacings of onion and those old time
green beans we boiled with bacon
before the magic of herbs

    2

town library this busy afternoon
we take the elevator
following four teenagers
tall and lean they will live forever
perhaps now they are come reading
before basketball practice
or maybe they have the afternoon off
a tournament upset this last weekend

old man wanted to go down
but the cage rises the point guard
working the button apologetic
says he did press basement the old man
telling him it does not matter
his old time is not valuable anyway
and the point guard sings nearer to heaven
as we spill out on the third floor

3

here is a room for artists
woolen moon on the horizon
stitchery of three rivers below
a pair of smoky eyes in a blue atlantic
comfort of africa I read
and remember a bell buoy
clanging in the wind off oregon
catcalling of the effortless gulls
my pacific and darkness ahead under fog

4

this gray afternoon we walk
bricked streets in the lincoln home area
persistent chiming the light breeze
troubling the frostbound hardwoods
1860s houses all painted up now
it was not so in the 1970s
old paint peelers then
and becky had her first floor apartment
and good popcorn parties
exhalations of cigarette smoke
I remember standing on her porch
looking north and the lincoln home there
a voice muted in the darkness

becky had her tall windows
hung with bedsheets she was
a clever seamstress this was before
the park service reclaimed the old homes
and where becky lived this is
headquarters for a congressman now

   5

so my personal lincolnalia
involves poets and eager fiction writers
etching their small histories in that place
our time has come so much to honor

reclaiming the light

now as to great grandmother
she would have been the poet
but in ireland she would have
hidden her talent and so
I do not find her in the solemn
anthologies and for a likeness
if there ever was one
a snapshot even I dont have it
she might have looked like my brother
with his blue eyes or like
my daughter who reclaims
for my wonder a particular smile
my mother had that was contraband
within the cargo of her vexations
and so whoever great grandmother was
I cannot make her reappear
as a beacon in a distant place
or as a banner I can claim for myself
it is rather that she is a lamp
perhaps a tiffany soft toned and delicate
with her packets of rhymes
I imagine she brought to her day
I who speak of her from compulsion
prophet or outlaw with my words
she is the abandoned life
the sign for me that was lost

peace store

1

a universe under this
overhead fan some cool
heaven here a rabbit ear mask
a grumpy lion buttons forming
a peace sign some of them
less than peaceful a hollow square
hung with the worlds
bright earrings and here are
purses woven in guatemala
if there is terror in their making
it is not showing in these
pulsations of color
and how fine these bowls are
even the crude beginners attempt
why does it inspire reverence
rainbowed covenant of clay

2

start the year right
with bumper stickers
where is survivor the cat
she would have been
the best of companions
she always visits with a purpose
all the twelve-step people
come in to love survivor

3

this new map of the world
how large saudi arabia is
could fill up a good
quarter of china and we are
US between the seas
compact we would fill
no more than half of africa
from tunisia to nigeria
yes northern nigeria and
on the horizon east to west
from somalia to mauritania
this is the corrected map
one in equal area presentation
it is strange face to face
with sudden limitation as if
there were no flag
two-blocked at the masthead
unfurled for the pride in it

4

floor squares of marbled
black and white tiles
dusty from the parking lot
you can read the footprints
worth pondering the old toes
delighted or depressed in old shoes
and on the wall near the door
a finger drawing down an eyelid
for some reason or other
some imperium of death
or an agony that screams for life

goethes dog would have been sublime

there is no reason
for having a dog
get into this book of poems
but he is my dog
and now he comes over
he wants me to scratch his ears
invites me to itch that joint
where the master of dogs
has attached his tail

for bill stafford and pete simpson

now I open this book
from petes estate
and read back of the dedication page
"most mornings I will
find you"

only stafford
would have penciled
a message like that
he was something
more than the world

and his book from 73
was a present for his friends
and for pete and myself
and for you as he said

especially for you

the mahotella queens and mahlathini

these old women who would have thought
they would dance all night like that
well these dancing ladies they couldnt be
more than fifty but that is old enough
I cant believe it the tireless shagging

and mahlathini he has a voice
he must have dug in a cave for
all those feral hoots and grunts
the women keep stage right
they have some reservations about a man
moaning at them in a leopard skin

but now look how one of the queens
matches him step for step in her furious
tennis shoes and now the other three
mock at him with their old zulu moons
and they are all a dazzle of shimmy and whistles
and the audience is stunned in the light
and flash of guitar and bass and sax

and its put on your dancing shoes
come on in with your sacred spaces
come on in here and be dangerous
and its yes yes yes yes yes yes
YAAvoh YAAAAvoooh YAAAAAAVooooohhh

after the pancakes and the shouting

how can we mask what we feel
the eye weeping in the hand
earth and heaven and all
beneath the earth
shards broken on a table

too soon what is there to say
parable of the workers
hired hands the first and the last
small pennies the least tax
left on the counter after change

lonesome in the book of midas
even the millionaire his social club
that sad need and here envy
puffing my small pain
what is it I desire

council ring bridge fountain
prairie restoration stream boundary
coming home glide of some melody

motes of dust in the windowed sun

you know it was a day
of long silences
something turning us inward
we have to contend with

I was up after midnight
waiting for the fire to die down
the last fire of the winter I thought

as I banked it under ashes

rendering the maple syrup

sun on the lake
a hesitant migration
the trail here is clearly marked
we walk on woodchips
they cover frozen loam
surface soft with a recent thaw
small ridges of snow and ice
shadow lacings beneath the trees
this long winter this too long
winter and a little warmer this day
and the wind still so that
everything seems poised
all stark between the cold
and a drowsing spring

we pass a man sitting on a bench
a great bodied old man
with a face full of flames
like a sundown or a sunrise
why is he here perhaps he is waiting
for grandchildren they are
crowding the garden shelter
pressing around a guide who tells them
the february syrup is darker
the maple in march more translucent

what is the inscription
on that bench with the old man
man with the lollipop in his mouth
we will determine what is to be done
and learn how to do it
and see that it is done

smoke from the wood fire
billows in white clouds
from beneath the cauldrons

the sorrows of the marsh arabs
and the mind running on

there was joseph jagger
he broke monte carlo
2,000,000 francs he knew
the wheel had a faulty spindle
he died of boredom

unamuno the basque philosopher
he was chancellor of salamanca
he said it was for his sins

mail today a package from diana
she sends strings of metallic beads
throws from the mardi gras
plastic necklaces in hot colors
tells me there are all kinds of throws
you can take your pick she says
cups doubloons panties stuffed animals
tells me how good the weather is
south in louisiana

well we have it raw here
stiff winds harrying the oak leaves
ice gleaming on the lawn
hanging in seed pearls from the elms
this is a bad time of year
when the burdened trees crack
and the night is an insane artillery
or a silk gown loosed from the shoulder
unsheathing a forbidden eden

what are you talking about
only that the day is short
when the ancient city goes down
and a father holds his shocked
sons and daughters in his arms

day of the butterfly conference

    1

marsh north of theodore road
canada geese and mallards
a raucous keyboard black on ivory
and a surprise of mergansers
hookbills chestnut headed females
the west wind sharp with winter
the sun easterly toward april
the morning an excitement of birds

these geese they say calling in flight
are the souls of unbaptized children
wandering the heavens until doomsday

some builder staked his claim here
his hundred thousand dollar homes
will have this wild scene for prospect
and the geese who will save them

    2

and now let us consider
the periodic table of the elements
we who are gathered here
somewhat ambiguously I mean
collectively or individually
without monoblasts and red bone marrow
and so I cite for example
K FE CO CU TI and all the others
for adding or subtracting
the material universe and rejoice
another day you will love the painted ladies
fluttering in sundrop prairies

3

single minded covey this morning
no makeup for the women
the men looking only just now
unzipped from their sleeping bags

4

this animal is monitoring
our college laboratory
it is staring above E-X-I-T
caribou with ornaments
dangling from its antlers
turn off the lights
it is speaking out of
the corner of its mouth
turn off the lights
its gold silver red blue green balls
all in a post holiday jangle
turn off the lights
this is the most serious
stuffed caribou in the world
it is saying pardon my dust
and turn off the lights
US Fish and Wildlife Service
Department of the Interior 1849 C Street NW
Washington DC 20240
turn off the lights
turn off the lights

5

the college has 120 acres
campus a priceless natural area
but who did it with his slide rule
designed these buildings
these stark blocks in the best
mussolini modern
anything would improve these eyesores
grafitti gang signs anything
oh some day let the genius come
who will paint these walls
vibrant with black dashes sulphurs
spicebush swallowtails coral hairstreaks
under this pale winter heavy illinois sky
anything that is beautiful

6

you need flashlights with powerful beams
red filters for the beams the moths
cant see in the dark but then again
a light too bright is abhorrent it is
the glowing moon they revel in
give them the moonlight and the dark
will zing with their exaltation

six yellow rectangles in a double row
on down the back and you have the hawk moth
they browse the petunia beds
suck the white fringed orchid
you can measure their tongues
unrolling them with needles
but it is not easy without a spell
they do not see red this is
why the flashlights have filters

7

illinois-michigan canal it is here
near morris city they call it the tree
that cottonwood from 1790
it lofted a hundred thirty feet in the air
would comfort twenty children
telling their stories in the bole
old shaman some great wind god you conjured
roared your medicine lodge down

8

at the rest stop on I-55
along the foundation wall
where the pfitzer junipers are
the kallay variety those shrubs
hide the big cocoons
of the cecropia moths the man dragons
with their seven inch wingspans
the ones they call robins
for their russet colors yes here are
the secret places for the pupas
until that small sum of seven days
when the moths will fly up
and remake themselves again

9

degraded oak barrens sketchy openings
where the lupines grow their pale offerings
palmate leaves radiant in their soft violet
she wolves feeding the larvae
destiny will transfigure as karner blues

it is the small black ants
that prize the nectar of the larvae
herding them at night among the blossoms
and bringing them safe with dawn
where the roots will be their shelter

nabokov named the karner blues
and so those professorial ants
imagine their gallic despair
when the larvae hasten toward easter
and loft on their blue hallowed wings
lolitas that will never keep in touch

10

all the best this year
all the best for the maple
each winter into spring
old family in funks grove
heft of the pint bottles
gleaming with the thick syrup
sweet smell of the rendering
the out buildings the windows
a warm glow in the soft night
this solemn stand
this dark good place

march and the crocus cluster

now here are these
blue marking pencils

blue petals in sixes
and the light pooling
deep inside

golden shallows
sanctuary candles
they are daybreak welcomes
for the inquisitive bee

chalices for mice

keen orange pistils
trifoiled from triple stamens

nuns in blue eye shadow
clinging to old habits

hunters trailing east
over tundra

small ones with small days

now a crocus mount st helens
rods a morning rigid with frost
snapped

but another generation
comes on in its own hour
spry as a boodle of kittens

they are a municipal band
ready for a park filled with thursdays

they bless this yard
year after year

and bless the girlchild
who will pick them for her teacher

there were choices

yesterday we spliced a video
bits and pieces
for a lost friend or perhaps her friends
she had a genius for friends
and now this morning
richard nixon put to his rest
those strained tributes
that california sullen sky
background noise the ceaseless traffic
I am sorry about this letter
I have never been good at letters
too self conscious my writing
too much given to acting
but let me continue there was
a dream I had once how I was in a theater
standing in the wings
it was a nineteenth century palace
baroque decor the good acoustics
and out in the dark house
a great audience mouthing its restlessness
and I understood
I had come there to play hamlet
a part I had not thought to study

AMI at the hilton

happy birthday
these twenty years and the
old wounds and
who is speaking to me there is
such pain reserved in those people
gathering around the tables here
something behind the smiles
the outreach what they share
so deep you cannot touch
so close to your own tears

from the podium
we hear about looking forward
about real team spirit
handfuls of dead words
a sad language but even at best
how could the language be
adequate and those who spoke
proffered their best
it is all right all right

bucking time for parity
we want what is good for everybody
and since when have our lives
been easy we were not expecting
unicorns browsing flowers in the yard

old wounds the stigma that does not
heal we would plunge that child
into resurrection well here now
complete the evaluation forms
give us your message at days end
the blood level determined
these heavy eyes
our limited resources

and now the young man speaks
and we know there are offerings
they are always
at the edge of things

polycarp

the city of smyrna
bosnia of its day
and wherever else
our murderous desires are

better not to know
nuances of hate or the cruel
need to preserve a self
down a hundred generations

better remember the victim
his shattering
his bodys sharing

his prayer for us

he was the incandescent man
an oven as they said of him
his death fire his sheath until
his captors broke his heart with a spear
and his agony turned to ashes

his hallmark was forgiveness
they came for him in darkness
it was long toward midnight
and so he gave them wine

and he fed them

*chanting the circle: lines
for earth week and the "greenman
is coming" pageant in carpenter park*

face the east
turn to all beginnings
all worlds that will be
made whole again
sun dazzle in the childs eyes

turn to the south
blush of hollyhock and the
red dirt there
all that grows in the
strengthening heat of the day
sweep of the fragile
swallowtail wing
new laughter and the
healing of old wounds

the west now
blue shimmered world
vanishing day
glitter of sunlight still warming
the closing eye
nailed tree of promise
and all our hope

now look to the north
gold sheen of the arctic sun
the long story
told in a snow trapped season
patience of seed
and the hands of love

and east again
completing the circle
under the heavens
their dark polish
a rush of all color
beneath our sandals

come around this circle
come around this circle
honor this world
and its six directions
and come on down
around again right

leland hotel a collage

what used to be the ballroom
they converted to a theater this was
early in the seventies and
guy roman did marat sade there
and the crucible they were
memorable in the round he began them
with a clapper so demanding
an entrance and if I recall
marcia lee was a little bit of a ham
giving us her fathers poems
that old lawyer offering in spoon river
everyone in the graveyard a day in court
and if I am not mistaken
the solarium above capitol avenue
that became an unkempt office
for the famous springfield gumshoe
robert miles he could look
from the west windows and see
the french empire dome of illinois
and then there was a room for readings
a little group cross legged
around jerry rothenberg
and he singing his beaver song
made up when the seneca adopted him
all I wants a good five cent cigar
over and over that good mantra
and there was a watering hole
john l lewis would hunker in
after he came on the train from lincoln
reading the iliad in the club car
old steam whistle moaning on the night
and vachel lindsay scratched his poems
sunny mornings in the tea room
and cyrus colter a formal dignity
took the elevator to the ninth floor
and chaired the commerce commission
with the brothers karamazov

tucked away in his suit coat pocket
he told me once in norb andys
and adlai graced the ballroom one evening
you know his concession speech
how he had it from lincoln
the little boy who stubbed his toe
he was too old to cry
but it hurt too much to laugh
so now my collage is pasted together
I hope it is more than what it says
more than the sum of its parts

humanities lecture at
the governors mansion on the
feast day of the venerable bede

it was a sunny evening
and we came from everywhere in illinois
for the lecture and the buffet
and the soft drinks and the chance
meeting with old friends
and to be told how we missed the cold war
the new world grown so unstable
better the ukraine held its missiles
with an iron fist or else the new
germany would hatch its own bombs
small pawns to counter the new russia
and it would be the same for japan
what with north korea the new
sundown in the pacific and well
this was the nub of our
humanities lecture on may 25
and we all raised our hands and applauded
shouting our alleluias for all our old world
the muffled drums the ancient tears
the universe swirling down one rod
when the last eye blinks
the rag doll for the goodwill box
with her embroidered heart

after the nuclear assurances

    1

where have we come from

strange men
lost in the moonlight
wanting to know
what happened to our children

heart stabbing anger

the free man
would have freed everyone

fire in the hearth
fire in the hearth

    2

what did it matter
the terrible death

we were sick inside with it

what did we believe
what did any of us believe

the blind sky
the lost moon
a blaze of orange silence

what did we see

and now the four seasons

    1

this day that was summer

a second and a quarter
fifteen hundred miles an hour
light winging
from the moon

a child at midnight
clutching a blanket in his arms

summer evening
riffled with fireflies

a gentle time
fan humming on the floor
three girls dancing

the river emerging
from green shadows
where sentences

have always been gardens

    2

autumn in illinois

it is all pastels

soybean fields russet
softening into gold

air quicksilvered
easy haze in the blue

white clouds in puffs
and the wind cooling

endless corn rows rinsed

barns and farm houses along
route four south of chatham
etched in the morning

thank god for these hours
a slow time this harvest

   3

beyond the cold solstice

canceled earth
a burial lights ambiance

our buttress in space

light bending around corners
feeding on emptiness

time chiming in us
with metaphors of bells

and now these waxwings
crested olives the impudence

see it is us us it is us

we are eating
your lacquered red berries

4

spring tokens

dogwood its repetitive
debate with april

fragmentary winds
breathing from the gulf
the yearly assembly

lovers once more
triumphant with their
begging bowls

earrings
hanging on a grin

the lonely woman
reads a small poem
by liu yuki

a heart breaks a stone

was a good party

you could sit on the porch in back
look left at the neon half moon or closer
where the musicians are within themselves
trumpet tilted high and straight shouldered
sax leaning forward in a confidence
drumsticks shaken loose from a pair of hands
who are all these people what is this
house with a limo long as a city block
artifact in the street lit up to the nines
why this is the house of the parrot
red beak red perch blue head green wing
glowing at the shoulder
a whole window audacious in neon
and here this surprise the UMW magazine
on the tank top in the bathroom
I do not know most of these people
their congenial and incessant murmuring
and most of them do not know me
as you would expect but look now
pictures on the walls wherever you glance
say now this one a man nothing but shades
and here off the open kitchen
a big yellow horn in a big brown hand
and you know this is a place
for the denizens of jazz and this party
a tribute shouted against time
for jim and kenny and fred
and whatever time can do
and for this moment we know the best of worlds
or one so close in the keyboard riffs

lines for the fourth

    1

you can see a lone rocket
off in the distance over the lake
sometimes or you can go downtown
not every year perhaps but
sometimes and you can watch
the angeled sky
dissolving into smoke
that curls in the slow summer wind
until the last spark is out

we used to have pancakes on the fourth
but that is over with now
our children all in their thirties
all away shot off over the country
like so many roman candles

    2

they say if you can get around
back of the statue you can see
how the right foot
arches on the toes and you understand
that the woman is striding
beneath her upflung torch

the wind stirs the sycamores there
and papery leaves dust liberty island

JULY IV MDCCLXXVI the raised torch
challenging a stubborn darkness
flame for prayers
liberty and order is it
possible our planet

this country this country
want it to be better than it is

3

chinua achebe in his wheelchair
brooding on nigeria says his country
cannot be father to him or mother
but only his child grasping for maturity

can the democratic society
be anything else

4

where is the convenient enemy
our necessary confrontation
the terrifying exactitude of our
righteousness what is left of that
when the enemy vanishes
a lost display in the midnight sky
and we are alone with only the hate
we need to destroy ourselves

5

I will speak of the news
just that the weather is mild
seasonable over most of the country
and that the day in town here
has been unusually quiet

*washington park
carillon festival*

timbre of these bells these old world
democratic holland bells
almost as silvered as russian bells
gates of kiev bells
here on a summer night
carillonneur fisting his keyboard
and his bells full flurried
roses blowing in the air bells
hour of the toccata and the fugue
hour of baubles and bangles
chimes falling like tears
bejeweling smiles in the peaceful assembly
on this sunday hedging on normandy
a half century ago and we are all
old men now who once impassioned
a savage world listen we did not
want to go out with death in our eyes
and now these quickening bells
oh hear them striking again and again

a little song for sugar cubes

he comes limping to my yard
with a mouth full of dreams

speaks of the dappled milkhorse
our ghost in the town square

the milkman had a blind daughter
he tells me this

her eyes were the blue hymns
of morning glories

where she walked
the stones wore purple

where she danced
the lightning split the elms

that was a long time ago he nods
I ask him where the years went

he smiles at the beauty of it
the angels opened a door he says

poems from vacations

    1

north carolina outer banks

fishermen from virginia
cursing the rays stab them
pink rhomboids one eye staring
a gold moon at midnight
the year toward midsummer the atlantic
rilling in golden breakers
the easy fall and heave of the sea
place for a slow healing
walking the hours on the beach

at kitty hawk the monument
thin spindle and rag crate
the wright brothers lofted here
so that we could tempt a further galaxy
so soon after

we have no time to repair
or test the consequences the grooved
stone ax thirty thousand years
we live by the half generation
roanoke island the earthen fortress
where were the houses what
happened to those settlers
why did this continent
swallow them up the child
virginia dare what became of her
and kim duk bay and moli canales
and maria transito mayancela
the little one speaking
the court language of the inca

2

south of fort worth

dizzying parabolas
wing flutter and glide of swallows
sixth street and west shaw
corn tassels waving over shrubs
leaves curling in the south wind
we are here it seems
in some other time and who
keeps the reckoning
this woman cant be late
she is running
her breasts heaving
her two sandaled daughters
pattering like raindrops
across the pavement
she has so many bundles

3

on top of the world

my adventurous daughter molly
when she was in the himalayas
met this hiker the other side of
thorung la pass and he told her
he was doing the world with his surfboard
but he left it in bangkok
when he went to the mountains
as there were no beaches on the
slopes of chomolungma
as it turned out he knew her cousin adam
often surfed with him in santa barbara

later when she was resting in bali
she was bit on the behind by an insect
she took a picture of the sore spot
shows you the advantage of photography

4

beneath kennesaw mountain

there was the diner
beyond marietta on the road
north for chattanooga
on the left I remember
and the country music
and bacon and eggs and grits
the road repair crew the dirt
embedded in their hands they were
polite to the waitress I guess
they had some south in that

they were tired there was
this look Ive seen it before
washed out these men
overworked on good wages
too much overtime and then
the job folding and what then

the man at the gasoline pump
did us a favor greased a stuck
handbrake he was from
rhode island said how he loved
atlanta the action in it
and all that passion for the future

I drove for my life on the freeway
everybody manic on the freeway

5

rafting in denali

river running gray its rapids
snow melts without oxygen in denali
mount mckinley in an anthem of cloud
well this was a float trip
three rafts and a water fight
nine women among others
hurling buckets and shouting and laughing
like girls released from the convent
for the parents day picnic
but tell you the truth they were
ladies of the anchorage evening
come cheerfully north on vacation
I think you should know this because
sometimes life is like that
and besides they called me pops

chinkapin oak
lincoln memorial garden

this ancient of days was a seedling
when the french settled in illinois
and that hour the widow of revard
the widow of etienne they had
all customary rights by formula
their village husbands held
notarized in documents according to
the usage of paris I am told

they were voting townswomen and did not
lose all that to maturing sons
so it is not a surprise we would have
the will of maria aramipinchic8e
daughter to the sachem of all
the kaskaskias and mother of aco
she was the wildcat who prayed
as we might say of her name

this oak shouldering the light
of a summer morning reveals
a balance of I-beams or some moment
soft as a tamaroa ribbon skirt
the ancient boundary marker
held over from the seventeen hundreds
it is more than the imagination
I have seen a woman leave the trail
seeking it with her hands
something pulsing within it within her

when the afternoon is waxing
the light takes comfort in the oak
resting within the great branches
and beyond the lake is clear and silver
spauldings dream the 1930s approved
with its seventy miles of shoreline the
socialist power plant the women funded
happily at the polls
despite their cautious husbands

comes the evening and the light
fading the oak is its own sufficiency
this is the hour of the fox and the raccoon
the doe leading her fawns

poet in a small place

sometimes he writes
almost spur of the moment records
like the seven oclock amtrak
wailing for the crossing
but then there is the life stance
the small town rural marriage
he farms it somehow
whether it is good or bad
it is not just a personal statement
he picks it up from the town itself
where death is a stone in a pond
and each house defines
the solitude in every window

oak ridge cemetery

she said the vietnam memorials were never lonely

breath of my choked word
forgive me
I have no defense
a cramped mind in the
knuckle of the world
let me apologize

I know that one person grieving
can fill the universe and that
what has been taken is gone
all the days that life
serves its poor bread

but there were in vietnam
two million casualties

and it is different there
the grief with so many
so suddenly taken so unpropitiated
wanting to return

we are abandoned to our anger
and the heavy lump of sorrow

but they live with the sundown dead
the hungry lost souls
in their ragged splendor
who steal the children

considering the budget with isaiah

8-4 flex time
graduate and two undergraduate
thursday free if possible
class elections hours
available schedule letters
no probationary
faculty *put on right*
eousness I dwell in the hie
and holy try out
both ways a choice text
expand definitions
hours available again look dates
up *prophets I haue*
set watche men in the small
ache of greed computer
fruitless part of the
student assessment
thou weariest thi selfe
no contract feel a little
better thursday it will
be all right time for
raking the leaves the
bathroom drain is stopped up
have to check that

program meeting

he doesnt like breaking us up
well a lot of asshole comments

question raised as to how
pay for the electric typewriter

what with the twenty percent
lopped from the new years budget

any delay will probably be good
maybe an upturn by october

talking about quality and how
measure the worth of the program

we need the new girl to log absences
surely something can be done

half of us are nearly expendable
why doesnt some colleague drop dead

poem at the full september moon

it has been awhile
different lives the worlds business
so we have drifted apart
shouyi and I he returned to
harbin china there in the north

we translated tang and sung poems
the old administrators
oh they could tell an emperor
a thing or two if an emperor
would listen and yes they understood
the slow ache of sorrow
departure brings to memory

so here I am in a jade evening
and the late tender light our sun
gone west with all his ribbons

this is the soft hour
for each in each the fine balance
where nothing need be spoken or denied
hour of the tree frog and the cricket
the easy movement of the elm leaves
sparrows peaceful in the black spruce

I think of shouyi far away
his busy stride beneath the moons
slow promenade the golden
shimmer of her dark silks
and what he would say this night
were we together why old friend
what meaning can we give our world

labor day this hundred years

how is it possible
this national holiday would have
grover clevelands sanction
labor honored in the breach I guess
and we are here between summer and fall
an overcast and clammy day
and all of us waiting for the predicted
afternoon pregnant with sunshine
it is a little more difficult
celebrating this year you understand
what with the flags the parades
the town picnics and the raffles
peabody shut down #10 in july
and three hundred miners
roofbolters and all went down as well
and in decatur the lockout goes on
the homegrown company town benefactor
taken over and soured

I remember the night shift
wham of the cutter in the mill
how you waited on the frail light
before dawn and the noise of sparrows
or forking sixteen ounce cans into boxes
eight hours a day forty a week
or digging postholes in a six man crew
and I know what those
stalled bargaining sessions mean oh yes
so many open graves

have you been to el paso
have you seen the razor wire
looked across the rio grande to juarez
oh banditos in the canyons
oh banditos in the boardrooms
and who can drink the water
oh the days of the unions are over
sing the multinationals
dreaming of golden parachutes
have you been to the factories in haiti

this is the time for brothers
and for sisters in the soul
time for the blind man to open his eye
time when hunger is no longer a prayer
friends let us go on
let us take the good path
let us help one another
the orchards are filled with apples
we will slice them
and dip each slice in honey
and we will know how to
consecrate the day and the hour

double puppet

the puppet from nepal was broken
so I repaired it with glue and twine
now it revolves under its hook
blue shiva gives way
and yellow genasha appears
and shiva again and genasha
faster and faster until
black mustache and white fangs
whirl through white tusks and red trunk
and which has become which
not even john pell could determine

bhaktapur dancers
wear the trappings of such puppets
the nava durga spinning the evil flesh eaters
reduced to marionettes once
by a wily priest

all this is something to consider
because in the shadows of my dreaming mirror
I have outlived my life
and I do not know who will be free
or who will nail himself to the wall

gandhiji

wrinkled old man merlin of a
dream weaver boulder
the seas could not grind down
reading his thoreau
letters from tolstoy
preoccupied with precedent
custom dishonesty in the honeycomb
frail jack for the giant of empire
and doctor king seeking india
always as a pilgrim because
this was the country of gandhi

and it may be he knew this tolstoy
"I sit on a man's back
choking him and making him
carry me, and yet assure myself
and others that I am
very very sorry for him
and wish to lighten his load
by all possible means — except
by getting off his back"

but he went beyond that writer
praying for the dignity
even of oppressors
calling us out of ourselves
far from justice to that moment
with no bearings no fixed point
only the bell buoy
slipped from its moorings
clanging in the drift of the sea

dark spaces
thoughts on all souls day

someone might live
even beyond one self and come
dreaming into the evening of his dream

entering his garden
without a thought in mind
much as a dancer spins with his eyes
focused on a point out there

does not see
stage prop or conductors baton
or the uncurtained
dark eyes of the audience

there are no surprises
yesterday in his garden
there were spring beauties

this is his freedom
the joy of the aged
the solemn moment before
everything goes down

it has to be that day
the stars do fall
and they will fall
so that we may grieve their passing

and perhaps
grow older than any flowering

bagatelles

****

le phoenix en mue doit monter
son echelle avec le dondiment
de canard which is to say
the phoenix in moult has to
climb up his ladder
with a ducks waddle

****

opposite sundown
two planets
on this day that was sunday
we have seen something

****

embers in ashes
the unsignatured fields

****

there will be justice
the heavens falling
the distance of a plucked string
through filiations of anger
where the lovers
take their small boats to sea
and the musicians whore
cleanses the light

****

dead rat on the floor
he should have run for office

****

there was that harsh light
when the armies wept
there was that breath of wind in the desert
bells of frost reordering the time
there was the ready made america
there was the dreaming paradise

****

we must turn back now
toads are wintering
underneath the garden
how the conscience mourns

****

cold takes the winter indoors
on the stung cheek

****

you keep striking these lines
otherwise you are dead
listen I will tell you
a dazzle of blue sapphire
shocks the earth
oh the chutzpah

moses ben maimonides
shelter us in a language
beyond our references
a blue sky penciled with lambs

    ****

inward silences
those we would speak to
who cannot answer
or will not
the hours have narrow eyes

    ****

why take risks on your own
give someone else your apple

    ****

secretary married a trout
the pisces pleased her
poems are tourists of the mind
objects study us
they are hidden in an album
she said this like smiles

    ****

always before morning
I remember forever
what was forgotten in me
there is the blue light
there is the sun
on the other side of the world

****

mozarts quartet in d major
the golden honeycomb

****

south wind in winter
shaking these streetlamps
old women
bending over daystars
fortunes in their eyes
the ancient hours singing

****

children are fires of temporality
flashlights lifted from the kitchen drawer

****

no chance to complain
no poets here

****

the incomprehensible teacup
looking back on a face
initial intentions wrinkled
like the palm of the hand
logical sequences taking root
at the bottom of a page
chance curled in its womb
at the edge of silence
word stretching the mind
murmur of the pierced heart

****

how could the wilderness strike back
not in one lifetime surely

wild plum flowering
hidden pond melting its ice

****

principle meridians tiers
range numbers base lines
fractional forties or eighties
government lots bench marks odd acreage
hundred and sixty acre rectangles
and that trouble with true north
the alderman is cracking his knuckles
it is never hard to be unfaithful
like the fingers of a broken hand

****

mind at tenebre
all my life

shadow of a man
trying to sing

****

spindrift
a taste of salt

*some words for the lighting
of the christmas tree in the
auburn illinois town square*

this tree will be our own
rising star it will sparkle
even if there are clouds in the sky
this soft-needled fir
glowing with light
the greens blues reds
the yellows all
the good colors these
tinsel cheers in a dark evening

the winter wearing to that cold
hour when the snow swirls
may hide the solstice
and we will find once more the
vast dark of the first breaking
from which all the light
gleaming in our eyes was drawn

and so for those who will
come by and share these lights
and for those who have
lived here in our time
or back as far as the generations go
and for those who will yet
move here in some other season
of flickering lights
let us ask a blessing
a blessing for all of them
and for ourselves — and everyone

as we stand in the privilege
of this one instant prepared for us
on this small planet
this manger of reflecting light
in the freedom of the heavens

perspectives on aging
lines for an anniversary

1

what was that
someone slamming a car door
someone up early
with a purpose

maybe I should do something
breathe or something

2

did you leave your teeth
on the bathroom sink

no dear those were your teeth

3

she wanted to go west
count eagles on the mississippi
feel the earth rolling
beneath the gaze of those raptors

she was all blue spirits
a shimmer of mute hozannas
at the limits of the heavens

he saw the willows
leaning against the wind

this man and this woman
at the kitchen table
drinking their coffee
a basket of seven pears
and two white candles
on the table between them

   4

he dreamed a woman
he never married
divorced him and how
she made her life over
without him

when he woke
he stared a long time
at the bedroom wall
trying to remember
who she was

   5

mind in the word
sifting itself going
onto the brink that
interior silence
along the edge of the hours
before dawn and the warming
day its tremors
spilling over with birds

6

he told her how he
loved the way her hands
could do so many
things how they
arranged flowers in a
vase or folded some
small note in a letter

she had grown used to him
after all the years
and finding now
he could still surprise her
she turned to him
and taking his hands
she held them

7

let us say
we shared a good wine
and the bread
had a solid crust
and whatever love was
we woke to it
and in the late night
we taught it
never to be afraid
of shadows

in the december gallery

and here is the baptist the honey man
a head on a plate offered to salome
the nubile girl still in her baby fat
earning a death so cheap it could not
soften those pouting lips
and he was the wild one
his ancient holy eyes glazed over

his word in the blood and bone
no different from the word
gone silent in his mouth

word beyond all that is random
word of an oscar romero at his altar
who chanted those names the death squads would
have blotted out forever
word of a malmud taha that man
so old the strictures of allah
would have spared him his scaffold
his body hidden now in the sudan
word of a decency in south africa
dragged down into one more death
yesterday or the day before or after

this is the hour to name names
when the serpent descends like a tear
beneath the lonesome eye and the mask
speaks once more its exalted language
here in this pernicious moment
noonday of the bitter nectar
pulse beat of a kathie kollwitz
mother and child locked in a cold embrace
when strength destroys the innocent
and only herods of the earth are durable

the woman in the red silk coat
garment laced with golden filigree
she would have loved the collages
these sequins faux pearls eggshells glitter
she always understood
so much more than we knew

now the last is the first again

good times here braving the weather
the wind with a bite in it
but we are gathered downtown
east of the state capitol mostly
for our first night celebration
on this the last day of the year

you can listen to the string quartet
so formal in the great hall of the library
or the rowdy irish band from chicago
this side the sanctuary
still caroled with christmas evergreens
where the lutherans worship
or go to the armory for the stolid pipers
with their drones and chanters backing reels
for the kilted young girls
dancing on their toes their arms
overhead like shafted beams through clouds

or wander in the capitol rotunda
where the big swing band in the tall dark
plays those dear cheap songs
as graham greene used to name them
for dancers in their street clothes
partners in the slow affection of so many years
I hear sentimental journey
almost to the hour I first heard it
a solitary once in a quiet bar
this was in san francisco and I
wounded home between all my life
and this december moment toward midnight

this is the happy time
time for the brainchild readers
presiding in the supreme court building

or that old gray haired central illinois
master of the proverb intoning his
suck an egg today scramble one tomorrow

or you can wander to the armory again
where prince julius adeniyi all welcoming
prays down a blessing on the house
and his big drums from west africa
come slapped into a life that shocks
the high rafters awake
and listen as he tells the crowd
I will show you how I learned these drums
when I was just a child
and he volunteers a towheaded
three year old boy from the audience
sits the child in his lap sets the childs hands
riding his own hard wrists as the drum
sings a continent under his palms
and suddenly he slips his hands
from beneath the childs and the boy drums
without missing a miracled beat
and adeniyi will make us believers
does this again with a girl in braids
she is so confident her heart
pounding in the drum while that audience
those parents and grandparents
respond laughing and slapping their knees
and some of them in tears

and the moment of the last hour comes
and the p.a. system gives us handel
and the fireworks blossom in the sky
and we come into the new year with bobby burns
for the kindness of it and I take
the soft sweet kiss of all promises
because it is that time again
yes it is that time

waking at two a.m.

I have studied all of the pictures
and shown them to anyone who wanted to see them
and I can put the book away now

JOHN KNOEPFLE came to central Illinois in 1972 to teach creative writing and literature at Sangamon State University. He is the author of many books of poetry and fiction including *Rivers into Islands,* University of Chicago, 1965; *thinking of offerings,* Juniper, 1975; *poems from the sangamon,* University of Illinois, 1985; *Selected Poems,* BkMk Press, 1985; *Dim Tales,* Stormline, 1989; and *begging an amnesty,* Druid, 1994. Translations include *Twenty Poems of Cesar Vallejo* with James Wright and Robert Bly, The Sixties Press, 1962; and *Song Dynasty Poems* and *T'ang Dynasty Poems* with Wang Shouyi of Heilonhjiang University in Harbin, China, Spoon River Poetry Press, 1985. In 1986 Knoepfle was named Illinois Author of the Year by the Illinois Association of Teachers of English and received the Mark Twain Award for Distinguished Contributions to Midwestern Literature. In 1995 he received the Illinois Literary Heritage Award from the Illinois Center for the Book. A film documentary, *Inland Voyages: The Poetry of John Knoepfle,* directed and produced by James Scott, was premiered in 1995.